I0813319

Anything that can't be done in bed isn't worth doing at all.

—GROUCHO MARX

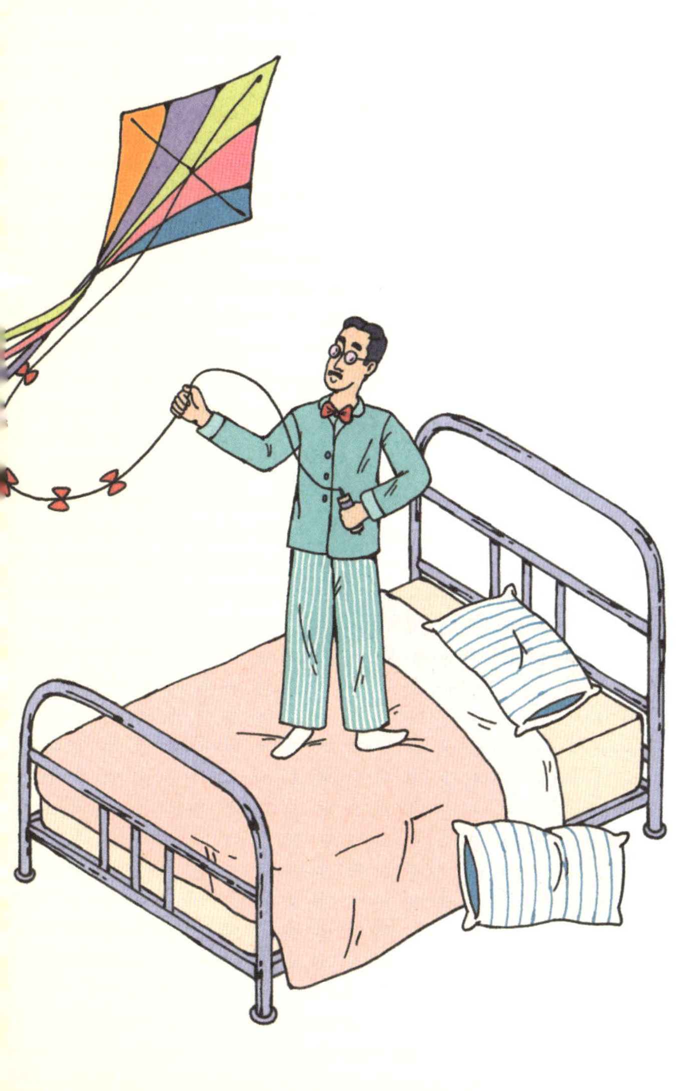

Created, published, and distributed by Knock Knock
6695 Green Valley Circle, #5167
Culver City, CA 90230
knockknockstuff.com
Knock Knock is a registered trademark of Knock Knock LLC

Printed in China

Illustrations by Kaitlin Brito

ISBN: 978-168349461-4
UPC: 825703503159

10 9 8 7 6 5 4 3 2 1

Cozy Hobbies YOU CAN DO *in bed*

KNOCK KNOCK®
LOS ANGELES, CALIFORNIA

And you thought hanging out in bed couldn't get any better!

LIKE ALL WARM-BLOODED ANIMALS, YOU WANT TO COZY UP IN BED AS MUCH AS POSSIBLE, RIGHT? Of course you do! It's totally normal. You also enjoy having fun and learning. There's no reason you can't combine all these passions . . . and there are all kinds of reasons why you should!

Certain people—including artists and writers—have always known that you can do almost anything in bed. The rest of us figured this out during the events of 2020. Your bed is a nest for sleep and rest and other nice things (if you're lucky). But it's also a creative incubator where you can more easily enter a "flow" state, the zone where time is suspended and things seem to come easily.

That's the zone where great art is made (and LOTS of great art has been made in bed) . . . but it's also the zone where a lot of great FUN is had—straight-up dopey, childlike fun, for no good reason besides having fun! That's what this book is about: being in bed—which is where we all want to be—while enjoying hobbies in your leisure time! This is the kind of extravagance our ancestors could only have dreamed of, and it's practically free! Why would you go anywhere but back to bed?

Now go on and live your #bedlife!

TABLE OF CONTENTS

Balloon Animals

Become the least-boring grownup in all the land (or on the block).

THE BASIC IDEA: Mesmerize kids and kids-at-heart with your god-like ability to create life from rubber!

THE WHAT: For too long, clowns have lorded their powers of creation over the rest of us. No more! The secret knowledge of making inflatable wiener dogs is for all the people. Just start simple, and give yourself a head start by using those long-and-skinny balloons made special for the job!

THE WHY: It's great for parties, satisfying & cheap! You could even make it a side-hustle!

HOT TIP: *The library has step-by-step guides & YouTube is a wonderland of how-to-make-balloon-animal videos. The whole world wants you to make balloon animals!*

EXTRA CREDIT: Make hats and cutlasses for a whole army of young buccaneers.

COZY HOBBY COMFY-COZINESS SCALE

LIKE A KITTEN · LIKE KITTENS WEARING SNUGGIES · LIKE KITTENS WEARING SNUGGIES SLEEPING ON A CLOUD

(Rating: 4 of 10, circled)

COZY HOBBY FYI'S

Do I need special tools?
(X) Yes ( ) No ( ) It depends

How cheap is this hobby?
( ) Free! (X) Cheap ( ) Not cheap

How asleep can I be?
( ) Super awake (X) Semi-conscious ( ) Fully zonked

Can I watch TV?
( ) Yes (X) Heck yes ( ) A thousand times yes

How much will I have to get out of bed?
( ) Never ever (X) Maybe once? ( ) Ugh like 3 times

Pilates

Tone up without getting up!

THE BASIC IDEA: Stretch, strengthen, and get some solid abs—in bed!

THE WHAT: Pilates borrows from ballet and yoga, focusing on core strength, alignment, and flexibility. Conveniently, it's largely done lying down.

THE WHY: Who knew lying in bed could be good for your posture? Pilates may not be as fun as other bed workouts we've heard about (ahem), but it's a snazzy way to start your day or wind down before sleep.

HOT TIP: *If you're a Pilates newb, check out beginner videos online. It's crucial to learn how to properly engage your deep core muscles. (Does that sound weird? It's not weird. Don't make it weird.) Then, go explore the exciting world of bed-Pilates videos, which are actually a real thing!*

EXTRA CREDIT: Add small hand weights to up the challenge! No weights? Wine bottles work OK too, plus then you can drink.

COZY HOBBY COMFY-COZINESS SCALE

COZY HOBBY FYI'S

Do I need special tools?

◯ Yes ◯ No ⊗ It depends

How cheap is this hobby?

⊗ Free! ◯ Cheap ◯ Not cheap

How asleep can I be?

◯ Super awake ⊗ Semi-conscious ◯ Fully zonked

Can I watch TV?

◯ Yes ◯ Heck yes ⊗ A thousand times yes

How much will I have to get out of bed?

⊗ Never ever ◯ Maybe once? ◯ Ugh like 3 times

Leaf Rubbings

Make gorgeous art with zero skills!

THE BASIC IDEA: Create beautifully delicate, highly detailed impressions of real leaves using preschool-level materials—and preschool-level skills!

THE WHAT: Get a leaf. Get a piece of paper. Then just rub a crayon or pastel over the paper, with the leaf underneath! Instant art.

THE WHY: Leaf rubbings are oddly satisfying, even for grownups. They make you feel as if you've done a professional drawing of a leaf. But you haven't. You haven't even gotten out of bed. Nature did all the hard work, creating the leaf in the first place. It's not fair, when you think about it. Nature works so hard designing stuff, and then people come along and just copy it.

COZY HOBBY COMFY-COZINESS SCALE

LIKE A KITTEN · LIKE KITTENS WEARING SNUGGIES · LIKE KITTENS WEARING SNUGGIES SLEEPING ON A CLOUD

(Rating: 8 of 10)

COZY HOBBY FYI'S

Do I need special tools?
(X) Yes ( ) No ( ) It depends

How cheap is this hobby?
(X) Free! ( ) Cheap ( ) Not cheap

How asleep can I be?
( ) Super awake ( ) Semi-conscious (X) Fully zonked

Can I watch TV?
( ) Yes ( ) Heck yes (X) A thousand times yes

How much will I have to get out of bed?
( ) Never ever (X) Maybe once? ( ) Ugh like 3 times

EXTRA CREDIT: Mix colors for added interest, use different kinds of leaves, or try colored or regular pencils! If you're feeling really fancy, use watercolor pencils and see how that looks!

Learn about the Stars & Stuff

Be the person who can identify celestial dippers & bears—from bed!

THE BASIC IDEA: Get to know your astral neighborhood—the sky where you live!

THE WHAT: You don't have to take a class to learn the names of the stars, planets, and constellations—you don't even have to get out of bed. With the right app, all you have to do is aim your phone at the ceiling to find all the nearby celestial bodies, day or night.

THE WHY: The sky is more entertaining than all the streaming platforms combined (and yep, that's a lot!). Plus, you can navigate your ship at night when you become an old-timey pirate!

HOT TIP: *Star-gazing binoculars are easier than telescopes and will also work for bird-watching! (Please see next entry.)*

COZY HOBBY COMFY-COZINESS SCALE

COZY HOBBY FYI'S

Do I need special tools?

(X) Yes ◯ No ◯ It depends

How cheap is this hobby?

◯ Free! (X) Cheap ◯ Not cheap

How asleep can I be?

◯ Super awake (X) Semi-conscious ◯ Fully zonked

Can I watch TV?

(X) Yes ◯ Heck yes ◯ A thousand times yes

How much will I have to get out of bed?

◯ Never ever (X) Maybe once? ◯ Ugh like 3 times

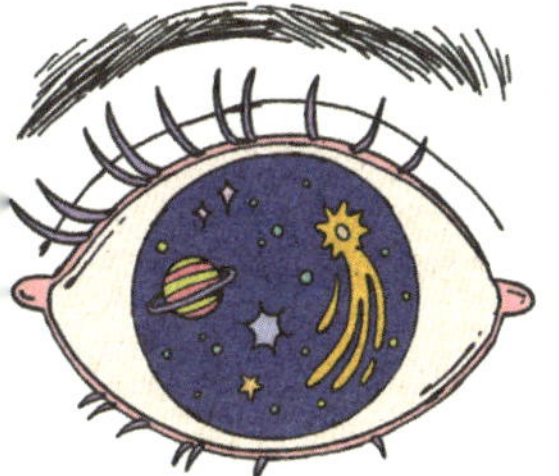

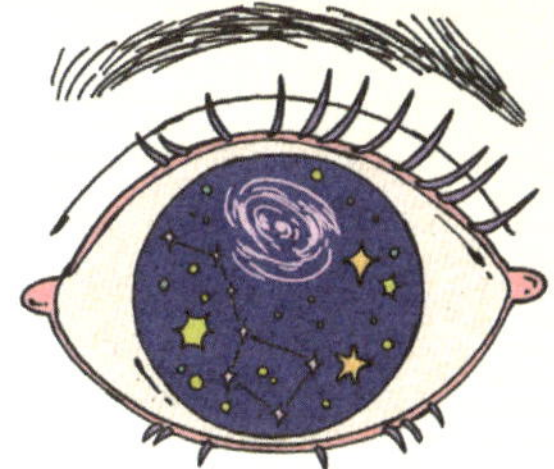

I am a completely horizontal author. I can't think unless I'm lying down.

—TRUMAN CAPOTE

Birdwatching

Observe flying friends from the comfort of your own nest!

THE BASIC IDEA: Look at birds and learn to identify them without getting out of bed!

THE WHAT: If you have a bedroom window, fantastic. If you have binoculars, even better! But if not, you can still birdwatch online, thanks to the wonder of "bird-cams." Yes, birdfeeders, birdhouses, and even birds' nests are tricked out with cameras so humans can spy on them 24/7. In a loving and non-creepy way.

THE WHY: Birdwatching is a hoot! Plus, it's healthy. A 2022 study found that seeing or hearing birds improved people's mental well-being for up to eight hours—for FREE! (Take *that*, therapy!)

EXTRA CREDIT: Learn bird calls using one of the wonderful apps available to help you record and ID birdsongs. At the very least, you'll always have something to talk to at the next neighborhood block party.

COZY HOBBY COMFY-COZINESS SCALE

LIKE A KITTEN — LIKE KITTENS WEARING SNUGGIES — LIKE KITTENS WEARING SNUGGIES SLEEPING ON A CLOUD

(8 out of 10 circled)

COZY HOBBY FYI'S

Do I need special tools?
○ Yes ○ No ⊗ It depends

How cheap is this hobby?
○ Free! ⊗ Cheap ○ Not cheap

How asleep can I be?
○ Super awake ⊗ Semi-conscious ○ Fully zonked

Can I watch TV?
⊗ Yes ○ Heck yes ○ A thousand times yes

How much will I have to get out of bed?
○ Never ever ⊗ Maybe once? ○ Ugh like 3 times

Make a Memory Box!

Preserve your good memories—without leaving your bed!

THE BASIC IDEA: Immortalize a vacation, era, or other special time in your life by putting things in a decorative box!

THE WHAT: Find a box that feels good and big enough, then decorate however you see fit. Paint it! Cover it with wallpaper! Write on it and in it! Place important objects inside. Maybe include some notes with relevant details, kind of like those descriptions next to pictures in museums.

THE WHY: Making memory boxes is easier than scrapbooking—plus, you don't have to smush anything flat! Plus, a memory box is like a time capsule. The older it gets, the cooler and more historical it feels.

COZY HOBBY COMFY-COZINESS SCALE

LIKE A KITTEN — LIKE KITTENS WEARING SNUGGIES — LIKE KITTENS WEARING SNUGGIES SLEEPING ON A CLOUD

(Rating: 10 of 10 — circled)

COZY HOBBY FYI'S

Do I need special tools?
◯ Yes ◯ No ⊗ It depends

How cheap is this hobby?
⊗ Free! ◯ Cheap ◯ Not cheap

How asleep can I be?
◯ Super awake ⊗ Semi-conscious ◯ Fully zonked

Can I watch TV?
◯ Yes ◯ Heck yes ⊗ A thousand times yes

How much will I have to get out of bed?
◯ Never ever ◯ Maybe once? ⊗ Ugh like 3 times

EXTRA CREDIT: Once you've made one memory box, think about making . . . another memory box! In bed!

Learn to Cast Rune Stones

Read fortunes like a Viking!

THE BASIC IDEA: Rune stones are used for divination and fortune-telling—kinda like Tarot cards, but with an earthy Norse twist!

THE WHAT: Runes are small objects inscribed with ancient Norse symbols, used for intuitive & cosmic guidance. For maximum soothsaying power, make your own runes from something natural like wood, rocks, or clay. Air-dry clay = EVEN LESS WORK.

THE WHY: Get ancient cosmic clarity, groove on the Tolkienesque vibes, and predict your whole future FROM BED! Plus, you don't have to be even remotely Scandinavian!

HOT TIP: *YouTube is an excellent beginner-friendly resource for learning how to make rune stones, what the symbols mean, and how to use them.*

COZY HOBBY COMFY-COZINESS SCALE

LIKE A KITTEN · LIKE KITTENS WEARING SNUGGIES · LIKE KITTENS WEARING SNUGGIES SLEEPING ON A CLOUD

(Rated 7 of 10)

COZY HOBBY FYI'S

Do I need special tools?

(X) Yes ( ) No ( ) It depends

How cheap is this hobby?

( ) Free! (X) Cheap ( ) Not cheap

How asleep can I be?

( ) Super awake (X) Semi-conscious ( ) Fully zonked

Can I watch TV?

(X) Yes ( ) Heck yes ( ) A thousand times yes

How much will I have to get out of bed?

( ) Never ever (X) Maybe once? ( ) Ugh like 3 times

GREAT MOMENTS IN (BED) HISTORY!

DID YOU KNOW?

Billie Eilish recorded her first album sitting on a bed. Perhaps not coincidentally, the album is called *When We Fall Asleep, Where Do We Go?*

Make a Little Book by Hand

Experience the power of making a miniature book—in bed!

THE BASIC IDEA: Create a handmade mini book with stuff you have around the house!

THE WHAT: You can make a book as small and simple (or big and fancy) as you like using paper, glue, a ruler, scissors, tape, and staples. You don't need to be talented at art or writing. But if you want to, go ahead and fill your book with words and/or pictures!

THE WHY: Handmade books are one of the coolest, sweetest, special-est gifts you could possibly ever give someone you care about. Plus, books are magic . . . so book makers are obviously wizards. Don't you want to be a wizard? Of course you want to be a wizard.

COZY HOBBY COMFY-COZINESS SCALE

LIKE A KITTEN — LIKE KITTENS WEARING SNUGGIES — LIKE KITTENS WEARING SNUGGIES SLEEPING ON A CLOUD

COZY HOBBY FYI'S

Do I need special tools?

○ Yes ○ No ⊗ It depends

How cheap is this hobby?

○ Free! ⊗ Cheap ○ Not cheap

How asleep can I be?

⊗ Super awake ○ Semi-conscious ○ Fully zonked

Can I watch TV?

○ Yes ⊗ Heck yes ○ A thousand times yes

How much will I have to get out of bed?

○ Never ever ○ Maybe once? ⊗ Ugh like 3 times

HOT TIP: *Search "how to make a mini book." The British Library has a supercute online tutorial!*

EXTRA CREDIT: Use your skills to make other things, like a garland of super tiny books! Christmas tree ornaments! Earrings! A bad cat toy! The possibilities are endless.

Jigsaw Puzzles

They're the new coloring books!

THE BASIC IDEA: Jigsaw puzzles come in all sizes and difficulty levels, and with a solid, flat working surface, they're great in bed. (No, that did not sound dirty. Let's move on, shall we?)

THE WHAT: Puzzles are having a "moment"—they're a tech-free, fun, affordable pastime you can do alone or with others. (OK, that kind of sounded dirty.)

THE WHY: Studies have shown that puzzles are good for your brain, helping with memory, relaxation, and focus. They're a fun way to get into a meditative "flow" state, and they're undeniably habit-forming—without side effects, next-morning regrets, or risk of STDs. (That was on purpose.)

EXTRA CREDIT: Try a 1,000-piece puzzle by yourself, or a crazy 3-D one! Invite the hotties over to show off your puzzle-building prowess.

COZY HOBBY COMFY-COZINESS SCALE

LIKE A KITTEN — LIKE KITTENS WEARING SNUGGIES — LIKE KITTENS WEARING SNUGGIES SLEEPING ON A CLOUD

(Scale of 10; 10th position circled)

COZY HOBBY FYI'S

Do I need special tools?

○ Yes ⊗ No ○ It depends

How cheap is this hobby?

○ Free! ○ Cheap ⊗ Not cheap

How asleep can I be?

○ Super awake ⊗ Semi-conscious ○ Fully zonked

Can I watch TV?

○ Yes ⊗ Heck yes ○ A thousand times yes

How much will I have to get out of bed?

⊗ Never ever ○ Maybe once? ○ Ugh like 3 times

Podcasting

Listen to yourself talk—
and talk and talk!

THE BASIC IDEA: Record yourself yammering on about your favorite subject—the more specific and obscure the better!

THE WHAT: Your cousin has a podcast. Your neighbor has a podcast. You're a fascinating person (way more than your neighbor, who's super-nice, but like, almost too nice?). If they have podcasts, why not you?

THE WHY: Bed's an awesome place to record yourself (especially if you throw blankets over your head and your mic). All that fluff acts like sound baffling in a real recording studio. Oh yeah, and podcasting is fun—with over 3 million active podcasts in the world (and counting), it better be!

COZY HOBBY COMFY-COZINESS SCALE

LIKE A KITTEN — LIKE KITTENS WEARING SNUGGIES — LIKE KITTENS WEARING SNUGGIES SLEEPING ON A CLOUD

(Rating: 3 of 10 kittens circled)

COZY HOBBY FYI'S

Do I need special tools?

(X) Yes ( ) No ( ) It depends

How cheap is this hobby?

( ) Free! ( ) Cheap (X) Not cheap

How asleep can I be?

(X) Super awake ( ) Semi-conscious ( ) Fully zonked

Can I watch TV?

(X) Yes ( ) Heck yes ( ) A thousand times yes

How much will I have to get out of bed?

( ) Never ever ( ) Maybe once? (X) Ugh like 3 times

HOT TIP: *There's a million ways to podcast (some people even do it on their phones), and a bazillion books, websites, and other resources for learning how to get started!*

EXTRA CREDIT: Start your own companion newsletter for your podcast, or start a podcast about the making of your podcast!

Reiki

Use your own life force to relax & pick up good vibrations

THE BASIC IDEA: Harness the "electricity" in and all around you to feel better! In bed!

THE WHAT: You don't have to be a Jedi to use the force. Reiki is believed to tap the earth's electrical field—and the body's life force, or chi—to support your own self-healing powers. But you barely have to move. It's like tai chi for super lazy people.

THE WHY: Scientists don't know quite how it works, but reiki has been shown to help relieve anxiety and depression, lower blood pressure, & boost immunity. (And, possibly, lift fallen spaceships from alien swamps!)

COZY HOBBY COMFY-COZINESS SCALE

COZY HOBBY FYI'S

Do I need special tools?

○ Yes ⊗ No ○ It depends

How cheap is this hobby?

⊗ Free! ○ Cheap ○ Not cheap

How asleep can I be?

○ Super awake ○ Semi-conscious ⊗ Fully zonked

Can I watch TV?

⊗ Yes ○ Heck yes ○ A thousand times yes

How much will I have to get out of bed?

⊗ Never ever ○ Maybe once? ○ Ugh like 3 times

HOT TIP: *Rub your palms together quickly, then hold them up facing each other but not touching. If you feel a vibration or tingling, that's your chi! Place one palm on your forehead and one on your chest/heart. Take a deep breath. Aaaaaaaaah.*

EXTRA CREDIT: With your chi revved up in your hands, try a short meditation with your hands on your belly and heart. Or battle a Sith while blindfolded.

PILLOW talk
All women should have a day a week in bed.
—EDITH SITWELL

Journaling

Let it all out. On paper. In bed!

THE BASIC IDEA: Write down whatever's on your mind—no topic is off-limits. Even *that* one.

THE WHAT: A journal is a private place to write down your thoughts, memories, hopes, anxieties, fantasies, dreams, etc., without pressure or prying eyes. (Unless you turn out to be famous, in which case everyone will read it after you die. But then you'll be dead, so who cares.)

THE WHY: Journaling helps reduce stress, improve mood and well-being, and even lower blood pressure. Writing about traumatic or stressful events is especially helpful, even if you only do it for 15 minutes.

COZY HOBBY COMFY-COZINESS SCALE

LIKE A KITTEN — LIKE KITTENS WEARING SNUGGIES — LIKE KITTENS WEARING SNUGGIES SLEEPING ON A CLOUD

(Rating: 10 of 10 — circled at "Like kittens wearing snuggies sleeping on a cloud")

COZY HOBBY FYI'S

Do I need special tools?
◯ Yes ⊗ No ◯ It depends

How cheap is this hobby?
◯ Free! ⊗ Cheap ◯ Not cheap

How asleep can I be?
◯ Super awake ⊗ Semi-conscious ◯ Fully zonked

Can I watch TV?
⊗ Yes ◯ Heck yes ◯ A thousand times yes

How much will I have to get out of bed?
⊗ Never ever ◯ Maybe once? ◯ Ugh like 3 times

HOT TIP: *Don't overthink it. Just grab a notebook and a pen or pencil. If blank pages bum you out, google journaling prompts—or invest in a guided journal. It does half the work for you!*

EXTRA CREDIT: Journal for 15 minutes, three times a week, for a few weeks. See if you notice any positive effects!

Make Pressed Flowers

So delicate. So pretty. So flippin' easy.

THE BASIC IDEA: Preserve the beauty of flowers and leaves with the power of gravity and time.

THE WHAT: Even a natural-born plant killer can create lasting tokens of natural beauty! All you need is some parchment or tissue paper, a heavy book, flowers, and patience. Flowers take a couple weeks to dry!

THE WHY: It's ridiculously cheap and easy to make these romantically nostalgic, gifty-type things for grandmas, kids, teachers, or perhaps someone you like-like!

COZY HOBBY FYI'S

Do I need special tools?
(X) Yes ( ) No ( ) It depends

How cheap is this hobby?
(X) Free! ( ) Cheap ( ) Not cheap

How asleep can I be?
( ) Super awake ( ) Semi-conscious (X) Fully zonked

Can I watch TV?
( ) Yes ( ) Heck yes (X) A thousand times yes

How much will I have to get out of bed?
( ) Never ever ( ) Maybe once? (X) Ugh like 3 times

HOT TIP: *To start, choose a simple flower with a single layer of petals, such as vinca or plumbago. Fold between parchment paper inside a heavy book and wait a couple weeks. Et voilà!*

EXTRA CREDIT: Once you have a pressed flower you really love, run it through a laminator to make a bookmark. Or coaster. Or a poster for a dollhouse. Or a decoration for a piece of snail mail. Or weird earrings.

Crystal Magic!

Tap into the majesty of rock!

THE BASIC IDEA: Embrace these glorious minerals for fun, self-care, and magic.

THE WHAT: Crystals are solid minerals forged in the earth over millions of years, believed to possess amazing powers (kind of like superheroes . . . but rocks). Hold them, meditate with them, tell them your troubles. They won't judge. They've seen it all. They're literally like 12 million years old.

THE WHY: Hold a quartz in your hand. It's cool to the touch (and somehow calming), right? Told ya crystals were cool! Whether you're a science nerd, witch, or just a fan of pretty rocks, crystals are endlessly fascinating.

HOT TIP: *Check out a book or online guide to learn which crystals are believed to possess the powers you're looking for! Calming? Clarity? Confidence? Sex appeal? There's a crystal for your every mood!*

COZY HOBBY COMFY-COZINESS SCALE

COZY HOBBY FYI'S

Do I need special tools?

(X) Yes ( ) No ( ) It depends

How cheap is this hobby?

( ) Free! ( ) Cheap (X) Not cheap

How asleep can I be?

( ) Super awake (X) Semi-conscious ( ) Fully zonked

Can I watch TV?

(X) Yes ( ) Heck yes ( ) A thousand times yes

How much will I have to get out of bed?

(X) Never ever ( ) Maybe once? ( ) Ugh like 3 times

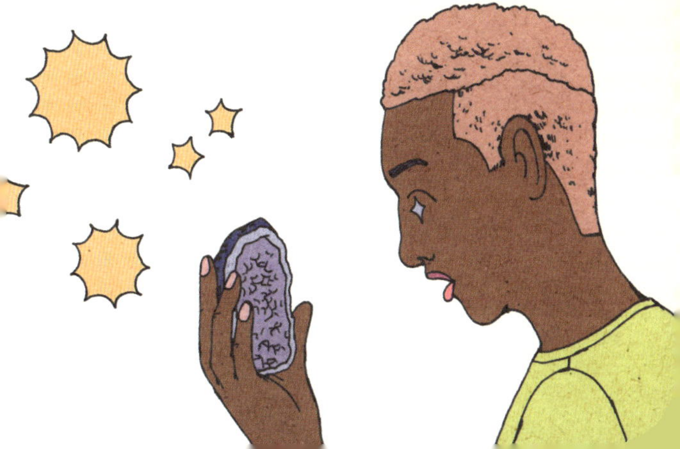

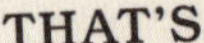

inBEDIBLE!

DID YOU KNOW?

Over the course of a lifetime, most people spend an average of 34 years in bed.

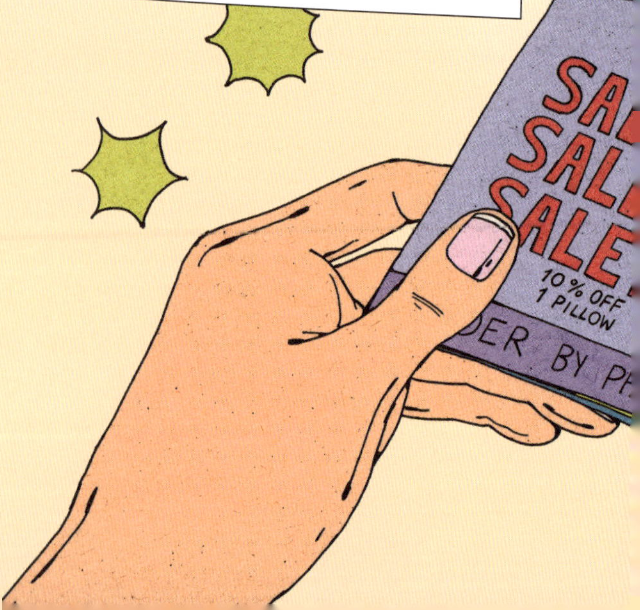

SUPER COMFY
BED WAREHOUSE
YOU + BED
TRUE ♥
→ AND MORE!
33 YEAR GUARANTEE!
1-800-SLEEP-4EVA!

Travel the World, Kinda!

See the sights without standing up!

THE BASIC IDEA: Visit places you've always wanted to see, while sitting in bed—just like the kids in *Bedknobs & Broomsticks*. Except instead of witchcraft, you'll fly with the sorcery of Ye Olde Internet.

THE WHAT: You'd probably like to go somewhere, someday, if you ever decide to get out of bed (which is not recommended). But you can go there now in your mind—without drugs! (Or with. Your call.) Besides being utterly creepy, Google Earth/Maps/Street View can take you to Machu Picchu, Stonehenge, and Easter Island.

THE WHY: It's like traveling, but without the expense, danger, smells, crowds, jetlag, luggage, language barriers, weird food, and homesickness. Why do people travel, again?

COZY HOBBY COMFY-COZINESS SCALE

LIKE A KITTEN — LIKE KITTENS WEARING SNUGGIES — LIKE KITTENS WEARING SNUGGIES SLEEPING ON A CLOUD

(7 of 10 circled)

COZY HOBBY FYI'S

Do I need special tools?
(X) Yes ( ) No ( ) It depends

How cheap is this hobby?
( ) Free! (X) Cheap ( ) Not cheap

How asleep can I be?
( ) Super awake ( ) Semi-conscious (X) Fully zonked

Can I watch TV?
( ) Yes (X) Heck yes ( ) A thousand times yes

How much will I have to get out of bed?
(X) Never ever ( ) Maybe once? ( ) Ugh like 3 times

HOT TIP: *Google "coolest places on street view" for shortcuts to some mindblowing adventures, including a crawl up the face of Yosemite's El Capitan from the perspective of world-famous daredevil climbers.*

EXTRA CREDIT: Use your discoveries to plan a real-life trip, down to the last detail.

Play the Stock Market!

Turn a little money into a little more money by just moving it around!

THE BASIC IDEA: Become a Wall St. power player—in bed!

THE WHAT: When you invest in stocks, you're making a bet that your money will multiply. Like all bets, it comes with a risk of loss. That's part of the thrill! Even so, if you're fairly careful, you're pretty likely to see your investments grow over time. How risky or careful you want to be is up to you!

THE WHY: There's a reason it's called "playing" the stock market: It's sort of fun. Wall St. is a giant game of strategy, instinct, and chance—except with real money. Thrill-seekers dig the risks & emotional highs and lows of following the market. Brains enjoy the intellectual challenge. And if you're woo-woo, it's a dandy way to hone your intuition and psychic powers!

COZY HOBBY COMFY-COZINESS SCALE

LIKE A KITTEN — LIKE KITTENS WEARING SNUGGIES — LIKE KITTENS WEARING SNUGGIES SLEEPING ON A CLOUD

COZY HOBBY FYI'S

Do I need special tools?

(X) Yes ( ) No ( ) It depends

How cheap is this hobby?

( ) Free! ( ) Cheap (X) Not cheap

How asleep can I be?

(X) Super awake ( ) Semi-conscious ( ) Fully zonked

Can I watch TV?

(X) Yes ( ) Heck yes ( ) A thousand times yes

How much will I have to get out of bed?

(X) Never ever ( ) Maybe once? ( ) Ugh like 3 times

HOT TIP: *First decide how much money you can risk losing, and whether you want someone else to do the work choosing investments. Open an account with a reputable brokerage firm—or go Lone Wolf of Wall Street via an online trading platform—and start playing!*

EXTRA CREDIT: Use your money to do some good in the world by focusing on socially responsible and/or eco investing!

Get a Pen Pal!

Make a friend without ever having to meet them, or get out of bed!

THE BASIC IDEA: Connect with someone across the globe (or across town) for the price of mailing a letter!

THE WHAT: Pen pal-ing has made a comeback since the pandemic. It's easier than ever to get started, and many organizations can connect you to pen pals of all sorts. (Grandparents! People your age! People abroad!) If you can only write once a month, NBD! No shame in that game.

THE WHY: If you had a pen pal as a kid, you may remember how exciting it was to get a letter from somewhere far away, hopefully with funny stamps. Some pen pals wind up becoming lifelong friends.

EXTRA CREDIT: Decorate your envelopes! Get more than one pen pal! Or start an Amnesty International letter-writing club!

COZY HOBBY COMFY-COZINESS SCALE

LIKE A KITTEN — LIKE KITTENS WEARING SNUGGIES — LIKE KITTENS WEARING SNUGGIES SLEEPING ON A CLOUD

(9 of 10 circled)

COZY HOBBY FYI'S

Do I need special tools?
○ Yes ○ No ⓧ It depends

How cheap is this hobby?
○ Free! ⓧ Cheap ○ Not cheap

How asleep can I be?
ⓧ Super awake ○ Semi-conscious ○ Fully zonked

Can I watch TV?
○ Yes ⓧ Heck yes ○ A thousand times yes

How much will I have to get out of bed?
○ Never ever ⓧ Maybe once? ○ Ugh like 3 times

DEAR

Learn to Draw

Sketch to your heart's content… in bed!

THE BASIC IDEA: Pick up a pencil and draw what you see, whether it's your foot, the cracks in the ceiling, or a passageway to another dimension!

THE WHAT: Drawing is a skill that's available to all of us, regardless of our "talent." Drawing is your birthright as a former four-year-old and human being. You don't even need a class or teacher, but you'll find an abundance of guidance and inspiration online and in books.

THE WHY: Drawing is calming, centering, and fun. It's free. You don't need fancy equipment. It's good for your brain. It's 100% real, analog, screen-free goodness.

EXTRA CREDIT: Give yourself a two-minute limit to sketch an object! Or sketch a famous work of art that you love! Do a self-portrait—in bed!

COZY HOBBY COMFY-COZINESS SCALE

LIKE A KITTEN — LIKE KITTENS WEARING SNUGGIES — LIKE KITTENS WEARING SNUGGIES SLEEPING ON A CLOUD

COZY HOBBY FYI'S

Do I need special tools?
( ) Yes ( ) No (X) It depends

How cheap is this hobby?
(X) Free! ( ) Cheap ( ) Not cheap

How asleep can I be?
( ) Super awake (X) Semi-conscious ( ) Fully zonked

Can I watch TV?
( ) Yes (X) Heck yes ( ) A thousand times yes

How much will I have to get out of bed?
(X) Never ever ( ) Maybe once? ( ) Ugh like 3 times

PILLOW *talk*

I always write in exactly the same place, which is sitting in my bed, with two pillows behind me. I've written fifty television scripts and two books on this one place on my bed!

—MINDY KALING

BEST TV
SHOW EVER
BAD
IDEAS
AWESOME
BOOK!

Strength Training

Pump Iron. Nap. Repeat!

THE BASIC IDEA: Get ripped, shredded, grated—or whatever the kids are calling it these days—from the cozy comfort of your snuggly-wuggly beddy-weddy.

THE WHAT: Using hand weights (or other heavy-ish objects), you can totally build your muscles without even standing up, much less leaving the house! TONS of strength-training moves are performed lying or sitting down, like chest flyes, glute bridges, Russian twists, scissor kicks, skullcrushers, and garlic presses. (OK that one's made-up.)

THE WHY: Consider how much time and money you'll save not going to the gym. It fairly boggles the mind! Bonus: You won't have to deal with other people's sweat & germs—or other people, period. Working out in bed saves wear-and-tear on your joints! Plus, you'll avoid the of tripping over barbells. (It happens!)

COZY HOBBY COMFY-COZINESS SCALE

LIKE A KITTEN — LIKE KITTENS WEARING SNUGGIES — LIKE KITTENS WEARING SNUGGIES SLEEPING ON A CLOUD

(Scale of 10; position 7 circled)

COZY HOBBY FYI'S

Do I need special tools?

(X) Yes ( ) No ( ) It depends

How cheap is this hobby?

( ) Free! ( ) Cheap (X) Not cheap

How asleep can I be?

( ) Super awake (X) Semi-conscious ( ) Fully zonked

Can I watch TV?

( ) Yes ( ) Heck yes (X) A thousand times yes

How much will I have to get out of bed?

( ) Never ever (X) Maybe once? ( ) Ugh like 3 times

HOT TIP: *Watch videos on how to engage your core and use proper form—it can make all the difference in getting ripped or getting injured.*

EXTRA CREDIT: Once you're done getting pumped up, do a whole session of stretching—in bed!

Learn a Language!

Give your pillow talk a dash of international flair

THE BASIC IDEA: Learn how to express yourself in another language, whether it's French, American Sign Language, or Swahili!

THE WHAT: Learning a new lingo isn't easy, but it's doable, especially if you're under a nice weighted blanket and sipping something delicious. Free online courses make it fun with bite-sized lessons and cute little animated characters.

THE WHY: Speaking another language makes you sexier and smarter. (Or seem that way, anyway!) It's a workout for your brain. It makes you a less-annoying tourist, helps you communicate with visitors from other countries, and might even make you a better job candidate! But really, it's the sexy thing. Isn't that reason enough?

COZY HOBBY COMFY-COZINESS SCALE

LIKE A KITTEN — LIKE KITTENS WEARING SNUGGIES — LIKE KITTENS WEARING SNUGGIES SLEEPING ON A CLOUD

COZY HOBBY FYI'S

Do I need special tools?

(X) Yes ( ) No ( ) It depends

How cheap is this hobby?

( ) Free! (X) Cheap ( ) Not cheap

How asleep can I be?

( ) Super awake (X) Semi-conscious ( ) Fully zonked

Can I watch TV?

(X) Yes ( ) Heck yes ( ) A thousand times yes

How much will I have to get out of bed?

(X) Never ever ( ) Maybe once? ( ) Ugh like 3 times

HOT TIP: *Turn off your internal editor and get comfy with making mistakes. Not being afraid to sound like a clown frees you up and makes the learning process way easier. Bed is a judgment-free zone, friends & amigos!*

EXTRA CREDIT: Watch TV or listen to the news in another language. In bed. Make it extra fun by ordering food (takeout, obvi) from the country whose language you're ~~butchering~~ mastering!

Genealogy

Discover your family tree, branches, and weeds!

THE BASIC IDEA: Learn about the hordes of now-dead people who all contributed to your history, hair color, health issues, and hangups!

THE WHAT: Exploring your roots is like being a detective, historian, anthropologist, and scientist all in one. And thanks to online databases, libraries, and DNA testing companies, you can do it while lounging luxuriantly in your happy place (AKA bed).

THE WHY: Discovering your ancestry can help you understand yourself, connect to new people & places, consider how the past has affected you, and generally trip out on the weirdness of existence. We come from Ice Age cave people and Neanderthals!

COZY HOBBY COMFY-COZINESS SCALE

LIKE A KITTEN — LIKE KITTENS WEARING SNUGGIES — LIKE KITTENS WEARING SNUGGIES SLEEPING ON A CLOUD

(Rating: 7 of 10)

COZY HOBBY FYI'S

Do I need special tools?

○ Yes ○ No ⊗ It depends

How cheap is this hobby?

○ Free! ○ Cheap ⊗ Not cheap

How asleep can I be?

○ Super awake ⊗ Semi-conscious ○ Fully zonked

Can I watch TV?

○ Yes ⊗ Heck yes ○ A thousand times yes

How much will I have to get out of bed?

⊗ Never ever ○ Maybe once? ○ Ugh like 3 times

EXTRA CREDIT: Treat yourself to some fancy DNA swab tests to find out where on the planet your people came from, and who else you might be related to!

GREAT MOMENTS IN (BED) HISTORY!

DID YOU KNOW?

Author Maya Angelou wrote in bed, usually renting a hotel room for an extended period and instructing the hotel staff not to change the sheets. She also enjoyed a glass of sherry in the morning when she was writing.

Animation!

It's actually pretty easy!

THE BASIC IDEA: You don't have to be Walt Disney to make a simple cartoon!

THE WHAT: Animation tricks the eye by flashing images so quickly they seem to be moving. Sounds elaborate, but you can do this simply by making a flip book with a sticky note pad! (It's also fairly easy to do on a basic computer.)

THE WHY: Animation is time-consuming, addictive, and ridiculously rewarding. It can involve playing with music, dialogue, sound, and writing, too—so it's kind of like several hobbies in one. And once you're done, you'll have a cartoon (or flip book!) to watch before your next movie!

COZY HOBBY COMFY-COZINESS SCALE

LIKE A KITTEN — LIKE KITTENS WEARING SNUGGIES — LIKE KITTENS WEARING SNUGGIES SLEEPING ON A CLOUD

(Rating: 7 of 10)

COZY HOBBY FYI'S

Do I need special tools?
(X) Yes ( ) No ( ) It depends

How cheap is this hobby?
( ) Free! ( ) Cheap (X) Not cheap

How asleep can I be?
(X) Super awake ( ) Semi-conscious ( ) Fully zonked

Can I watch TV?
( ) Yes ( ) Heck yes (X) A thousand times yes

How much will I have to get out of bed?
(X) Never ever ( ) Maybe once? ( ) Ugh like 3 times

HOT TIP: *You can make basic animation using PowerPoint & Google Slides. (Just google it!)*

EXTRA CREDIT: If you want to get a little extra, try a program like Stop Motion Studio to make a short stop-motion animation. Make clay figures, or put googly eyes on objects you have around your bed, like . . . a "talking" remote control, "dancing" pens, mutating pillows, etc!

Calligraphy

Write fancy like in olden tymes!

THE BASIC IDEA: Calligraphy is beautiful hand-lettering that can be created with a pen or paintbrush, or by using special calligraphy markers & such.

THE WHAT: You can teach yourself calligraphy by following one of many tutorials online. Pick a style you'd like to learn and begin with the alphabet. Don't be hard on yourself if it looks less-than-pro. Calligraphy is kind of like pizza—even when it's not very good, it's awesome.

THE WHY: Calligraphy is so beautiful, when people see elegant curlicues coming out of your pen, they'll think you're either a magical being or really cool robot. Win-win. Calligraphy jazzes up envelopes, greeting cards, gifts, labels, etc.! Who knows—if you get good, you could even do it for extra income! Some people pay good money to have swirly letters on their wedding invites!

COZY HOBBY COMFY-COZINESS SCALE

LIKE A KITTEN — LIKE KITTENS WEARING SNUGGIES — LIKE KITTENS WEARING SNUGGIES SLEEPING ON A CLOUD

(Rating: 10 of 10 — circled: LIKE KITTENS WEARING SNUGGIES SLEEPING ON A CLOUD)

COZY HOBBY FYI'S

Do I need special tools?

(X) Yes ( ) No ( ) It depends

How cheap is this hobby?

( ) Free! (X) Cheap ( ) Not cheap

How asleep can I be?

(X) Super awake ( ) Semi-conscious ( ) Fully zonked

Can I watch TV?

( ) Yes ( ) Heck yes (X) A thousand times yes

How much will I have to get out of bed?

( ) Never ever (X) Maybe once? ( ) Ugh like 3 times

HOT TIP: *Don't have time/energy to master actual calligraphy? Try faux-calligraphy. It's a legit technique! Here's how: 1) Write a word—any word! 2) Give the downward strokes a secondary extra-wide overlay stroke, making those bits of each letter thicker than the upward strokes. It may be "fake," but it still looks fancy!*

EXTRA CREDIT: Learn calligraphy from another part of the world!

Do Holiday Crap Early!

Keep the holidays in your heart all the year (in bed)!

THE BASIC IDEA: You can do festive stuff any time of year—crafting, menu-planning, shopping—without it actually being the holidays. There's no law saying you can't.

THE WHAT: Every year the holidays sneak up like a tinsel tornado, wreaking havoc and leaving a trail of shattered nerves and garbage in their wake. But if you're someone who secretly does enjoy holiday feelings . . . why not make an offseason hobby of it? Get your holiday shopping done. Create your own holiday cards. Make those acorn garlands you saw on Insta.

THE WHY: Seasonal activities are more fun when you're not super stressed, wondering how you'll get everything done.

COZY HOBBY COMFY-COZINESS SCALE

LIKE A KITTEN — LIKE KITTENS WEARING SNUGGIES — LIKE KITTENS WEARING SNUGGIES SLEEPING ON A CLOUD

(Scale of 10; 10th position circled)

COZY HOBBY FYI'S

Do I need special tools?
(X) Yes ( ) No ( ) It depends

How cheap is this hobby?
( ) Free! ( ) Cheap (X) Not cheap

How asleep can I be?
( ) Super awake (X) Semi-conscious ( ) Fully zonked

Can I watch TV?
( ) Yes ( ) Heck yes (X) A thousand times yes

How much will I have to get out of bed?
( ) Never ever ( ) Maybe once? (X) Ugh like 3 times

HOT TIP: *If you get some things done early, you'll be much less frenzied when December hits.*

EXTRA CREDIT: Since you'll have holiday stuff done early this year, why not give yourself the assignment of actually relaxing and enjoying the holidays—in bed!

Start a Newsletter/ Blog/Substack

Become an author overnight—in bed!

THE BASIC IDEA: You have stuff to say, and you deserve a platform to say it. Why not start your own newsletter?! They're a straightforward way to connect with other people via their in-box!

THE WHAT: Subscription newsletters are all the rage now, kind of a throwback to blogs but without all the popup ads and Comic Sans. Whatever your perspective or tastes—no matter how niche or nuanced—there are surely people out there willing to pay for 'em.

THE WHY: You get to make up a catchy name for your newsletter, and create a cute little branded icon for it. Haven't you always wanted your own icon?

COZY HOBBY COMFY-COZINESS SCALE

COZY HOBBY FYI'S

Do I need special tools?

( ) Yes ( ) No (X) It depends

How cheap is this hobby?

( ) Free! (X) Cheap ( ) Not cheap

How asleep can I be?

( ) Super awake (X) Semi-conscious ( ) Fully zonked

Can I watch TV?

( ) Yes (X) Heck yes ( ) A thousand times yes

How much will I have to get out of bed?

(X) Never ever ( ) Maybe once? ( ) Ugh like 3 times

HOT TIP: *If people like your stuff, you could make money just lying in bed, typing. What a time to be alive.*

EXTRA CREDIT: Make a companion podcast for your writing—yet another cool thing you can do in bed!

Everything is more glamorous when you do it in bed, anyway. Even peeling potatoes.

—ANDY WARHOL

Make Your Own Jewelry!

No one needs to know that bracelet was once a toilet paper roll.

THE BASIC IDEA: Make weird, cool, and (maybe?) beautiful jewelry using items that may already be hiding under your bed!

THE WHAT: You may know about using beads to make necklaces, earrings, etc. That's a valid way to go! But look around for other materials: coins, safety pins, paper clips, rocks, duct tape, foil . . . and, yep, toilet paper rolls. All these (and more!) can become eye-catching adornments.

THE WHY: It's fun, cheap, and it feels good not paying stupid amounts of money for unique jewelry you don't see everywhere!

COZY HOBBY COMFY-COZINESS SCALE

LIKE A KITTEN — LIKE KITTENS WEARING SNUGGIES — LIKE KITTENS WEARING SNUGGIES SLEEPING ON A CLOUD

(Rating: 7 of 10)

COZY HOBBY FYI'S

Do I need special tools?
(X) Yes ( ) No ( ) It depends

How cheap is this hobby?
( ) Free! (X) Cheap ( ) Not cheap

How asleep can I be?
(X) Super awake ( ) Semi-conscious ( ) Fully zonked

Can I watch TV?
( ) Yes ( ) Heck yes (X) A thousand times yes

How much will I have to get out of bed?
( ) Never ever ( ) Maybe once? (X) Ugh like 3 times

HOT TIP: *Ideas abound for getting started. Just type "make jewelry from anything" into your magical talking picture box with all the buttons (AKA phone/computer).*

EXTRA CREDIT: Learn how to make a ring, pendant, or bracelet from coins or silverware!

Do a Vision Board!

Create a picture of your dream life . . . and watch the magic unfold!

THE BASIC IDEA: Make an inspiring collage of images that represent your life goals. It couldn't hurt, and it just might work.

THE WHAT: Gather pics of things you want in your life—or that spark feelings you'd like to feel. Gaze at it daily. If all goes as planned, your life will start to resemble your collage! How, you ask? Is it the "law of attraction"? Magic? Um, maybe! At the very least, it's a fun way to spend another glorious night in bed.

THE WHY: Besides *they're cheap, fun & maybe magical*? Visualization has been proven to help athletes perform better—it's science! Plus, *what harm could it do*? Just don't use a picture of an interdimensional portal to a world of carnivorous robots.

EXTRA CREDIT: Make another vision board!

COZY HOBBY COMFY-COZINESS SCALE

LIKE A KITTEN — LIKE KITTENS WEARING SNUGGIES — LIKE KITTENS WEARING SNUGGIES SLEEPING ON A CLOUD

(9 of 10 circled)

COZY HOBBY FYI'S

Do I need special tools?

(X) Yes ( ) No ( ) It depends

How cheap is this hobby?

(X) Free! ( ) Cheap ( ) Not cheap

How asleep can I be?

( ) Super awake (X) Semi-conscious ( ) Fully zonked

Can I watch TV?

( ) Yes (X) Heck yes ( ) A thousand times yes

How much will I have to get out of bed?

( ) Never ever (X) Maybe once? ( ) Ugh like 3 times

Build Tiny Stuff!

Make an adorable scale model of a little bed—in bed!

THE BASIC IDEA: Build a diorama, model ship, eensy-beensy library, etc., either using a kit or freestyling from scratch! Miniatures are super popular, and you can find kits for virtually any interest or skill level.

THE WHAT: Anyone can build a lil' "book nook," model plane, mini flower shop, castle, T. Rex, and much more, simply by reading and following directions *very very carefully* and practicing great patience. Excellent lighting and good glasses also help.

THE WHY: Building miniatures is challenging and requires focus. It's super-duper-duper good for your brain, helps you access a flow state, and delivers a big bang of satisfaction when your project is done.

EXTRA CREDIT: Make a little community of miniatures, like a little town! You can be their all-powerful god!

COZY HOBBY COMFY-COZINESS SCALE

LIKE A KITTEN — LIKE KITTENS WEARING SNUGGIES — LIKE KITTENS WEARING SNUGGIES SLEEPING ON A CLOUD

COZY HOBBY FYI'S

Do I need special tools?

(X) Yes ◯ No ◯ It depends

How cheap is this hobby?

◯ Free! ◯ Cheap (X) Not cheap

How asleep can I be?

(X) Super awake ◯ Semi-conscious ◯ Fully zonked

Can I watch TV?

◯ Yes (X) Heck yes ◯ A thousand times yes

How much will I have to get out of bed?

◯ Never ever (X) Maybe once? ◯ Ugh like 3 times

THAT'S

INBEDIBLE!

DID YOU KNOW?

OK, we already knew this, but now it's official: According to recent studies, nearly half of Gen Z respondents say they often work in bed, including taking calls. Which makes them officially the most bed-rotting generation.

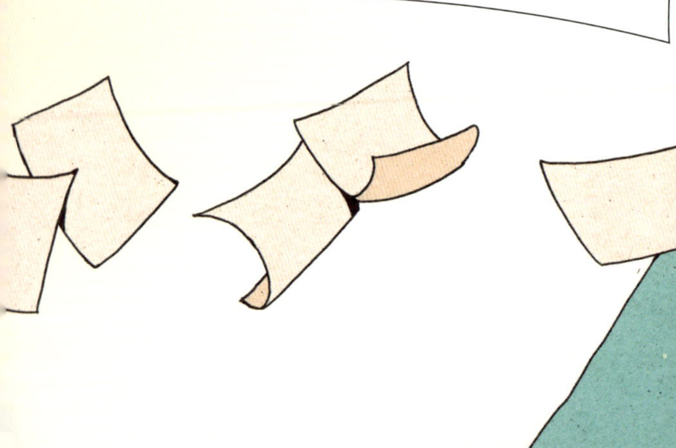

Make Candy Art!

Is there anything candy can't *do?!*

THE BASIC IDEA: You don't need paint or artist's clay to make deliciously colorful, textural artwork. You just need candy. In bed.

THE WHAT: Remember being a kid in a candy store? The dazzling colors, shapes, varieties . . . and the thrill you felt just *looking* at it? Candy is beautiful and makes delightful visual art! Make mandalas, mosaics, sculptures . . . whatever you can dream up.

THE WHY: Don't you want a picture made from candy? Of course you do.

HOT TIP: *If you plan to eat your artwork, use frosting instead of glue.*

EXTRA CREDIT: If you want your art to last indefinitely, be sure to look up some instructional videos! (You'll probably need to use a lacquer or resin.) Your art will look so good you'll want to eat it. Don't eat it.

COZY HOBBY COMFY-COZINESS SCALE

LIKE A KITTEN — LIKE KITTENS WEARING SNUGGIES — LIKE KITTENS WEARING SNUGGIES SLEEPING ON A CLOUD

(Rated: 8 of 10 kittens)

COZY HOBBY FYI'S

Do I need special tools?

(X) Yes ( ) No ( ) It depends

How cheap is this hobby?

( ) Free! (X) Cheap ( ) Not cheap

How asleep can I be?

(X) Super awake ( ) Semi-conscious ( ) Fully zonked

Can I watch TV?

( ) Yes ( ) Heck yes (X) A thousand times yes

How much will I have to get out of bed?

( ) Never ever ( ) Maybe once? (X) Ugh like 3 times

Host a Film Fest!

Can you throw a film festival without getting out of bed? Yes you Cannes!

THE BASIC IDEA: Curate an epic ~~binge-watch~~ film fest based on a theme! Get snacks! Invite others (or no one!) to watch with you!

THE WHAT: Choose a theme that fits your mood. If you're feeling blue or dealing with health issues, choose your favorite feel-good comedies. Laughter is healing—literally! If you're feeling dramatic, maybe go for film noir. Focus on a specific director, actor, or decade. Watch your favorite critic's top films of all time. And don't forget the snacks!

THE WHY: It's educational, entertaining, and even medicinal—and YOU DON'T EVEN HAVE TO GET OUT OF BED EVER!

COZY HOBBY COMFY-COZINESS SCALE

LIKE A KITTEN — LIKE KITTENS WEARING SNUGGIES — LIKE KITTENS WEARING SNUGGIES SLEEPING ON A CLOUD

(10 of 10 circled)

COZY HOBBY FYI'S

Do I need special tools?

○ Yes ○ No ⊗ It depends

How cheap is this hobby?

⊗ Free! ○ Cheap ○ Not cheap

How asleep can I be?

○ Super awake ⊗ Semi-conscious ○ Fully zonked

Can I watch TV?

○ Yes ○ Heck yes ⊗ A thousand times yes

How much will I have to get out of bed?

⊗ Never ever ○ Maybe once? ○ Ugh like 3 times

EXTRA CREDIT: Read up on the films you watch and their creators. Based on your research, create a selection of thematically appropriate snacks!

Make Pottery

Explore your inner clay artist!

THE BASIC IDEA: Make ornaments, candle holders, tiny mushrooms, or anything else you can dream of sculpting . . . in bed!

THE WHAT: Imagine yourself all cozed up and crafting away in your home pottery studio—AKA your bedroom! It's a good picture, isn't it? You can do this—without a class or pottery wheel! Really. Air-dry clay is a miracle substance. It's easy to work with and allows you to make all kinds of things. It's less messy than traditional clay and also relatively cheap. No kilns required!

THE WHY: It's shockingly simple to make cheap-yet-meaningful gifts & things. Even clay creations that look like they were made by a toddler with a caffeine habit are impressive to people who have never worked with clay.

COZY HOBBY COMFY-COZINESS SCALE

LIKE A KITTEN — LIKE KITTENS WEARING SNUGGIES — LIKE KITTENS WEARING SNUGGIES SLEEPING ON A CLOUD

COZY HOBBY FYI'S

Do I need special tools?

(X) Yes ( ) No ( ) It depends

How cheap is this hobby?

( ) Free! ( ) Cheap (X) Not cheap

How asleep can I be?

( ) Super awake (X) Semi-conscious ( ) Fully zonked

Can I watch TV?

( ) Yes ( ) Heck yes (X) A thousand times yes

How much will I have to get out of bed?

( ) Never ever (X) Maybe once? ( ) Ugh like 3 times

EXTRA CREDIT: After your creations dry, glaze them to jazz 'em up. There are loads of colorful glazes for air-dry clay and you can set up a little painting studio in bed—and keep your sheets clean—just by using a cutting board or other flat surface to work on.

Pet Grooming

They're gonna be on the bed anyway, right?

THE BASIC IDEA: Learn to groom your pet like a pro, without the cost (and humiliating hair bows).

THE WHAT: With Fluffy comfy on your bed, BAM! Brush her fur! BOOM! Trim her nails! It's part hang time and part chore!

THE WHY: Taking care of Fluffy or Fido's grooming needs is much cheaper when you tend to them yourself! And since it has to get done, why not do it in bed? Plus, if they're the kind of pet who gets freaked out by groomers, this will be a thousand times less trauma for them (and you?).

HOT TIP: *Keep a little basket of treats, brushes and pet clippers close by and when they stop in to check on you, lure them into a relaxing grooming session.*

EXTRA CREDIT: Decorate their collars or better yet, try to brush their teeth.

COZY HOBBY COMFY-COZINESS SCALE

LIKE A KITTEN · LIKE KITTENS WEARING SNUGGIES · LIKE KITTENS WEARING SNUGGIES SLEEPING ON A CLOUD

(Rating: 4 of 10, circled)

COZY HOBBY FYI'S

Do I need special tools?
(X) Yes ( ) No ( ) It depends

How cheap is this hobby?
( ) Free! (X) Cheap ( ) Not cheap

How asleep can I be?
(X) Super awake ( ) Semi-conscious ( ) Fully zonked

Can I watch TV?
( ) Yes ( ) Heck yes (X) A thousand times yes

How much will I have to get out of bed?
( ) Never ever (X) Maybe once? ( ) Ugh like 3 times

PILLOW *talk*

I do all my writing in bed; everybody knows I do my best work there.

—MAE WEST

Start a Book Club!

Talk about what you're reading with people who are interested!

THE BASIC IDEA: Find a group of friends who DON'T like leaving home as much as they DO like reading. Set up a video book club where you eat snacks and wear plot-themed pajamas, and get to discuss your latest literary passions.

THE WHAT: Like-minded people—ideally, friends!—who commit to reading one book every month (or however often you meet) and discussing it FROM BED! (Their own bed. Not one big bed. That would be a different type of club.)

THE WHY: The hardest part about book clubs is finding a time to meet that works for everyone. Once you move the club to video, no one will have to bother about finding sitters, getting off work in time, or brushing their teeth. Plus, you won't have to clean house before you meet!

COZY HOBBY COMFY-COZINESS SCALE

LIKE A KITTEN — LIKE KITTENS WEARING SNUGGIES — LIKE KITTENS WEARING SNUGGIES SLEEPING ON A CLOUD

(Rating: 10 of 10 — circled: LIKE KITTENS WEARING SNUGGIES SLEEPING ON A CLOUD)

COZY HOBBY FYI'S

Do I need special tools?
(X) Yes ( ) No ( ) It depends

How cheap is this hobby?
( ) Free! (X) Cheap ( ) Not cheap

How asleep can I be?
(X) Super awake ( ) Semi-conscious ( ) Fully zonked

Can I watch TV?
(X) Yes ( ) Heck yes ( ) A thousand times yes

How much will I have to get out of bed?
(X) Never ever ( ) Maybe once? ( ) Ugh like 3 times

HOT TIP: *Reading books and talking about 'em—in bed—is fun. Plus, it's probably better for your mental health than drinking boxed wine and doom scrolling for days.*

EXTRA CREDIT: Ask people to have a snack that relates back to the book, or have everybody suggest a song for a themed book club playlist.

Improve Your Cooking

You don't even need a kitchen!

THE BASIC IDEA: Get a stack of cookbooks or, better yet, binge-watch videos from a favorite celebrity chef. You can learn all kinds of tricks without getting out of bed!

THE WHAT: Just by reading & watching, it's easy to learn kitchen safety, meal planning, the history of ingredients, and cool tricks like making your own vanilla extract!

THE WHY: If you think about it, lots of cooking activities can happen outside the kitchen. Knife sharpening can easily be done in bed. Menu planning lends itself perfectly to lying down & daydreaming about food.

EXTRA CREDIT: Once you've created a meal plan, order your groceries online and choose a delivery time when someone else will be home.

COZY HOBBY COMFY-COZINESS SCALE

COZY HOBBY FYI'S

Do I need special tools?

(X) Yes ( ) No ( ) It depends

How cheap is this hobby?

( ) Free! (X) Cheap ( ) Not cheap

How asleep can I be?

(X) Super awake ( ) Semi-conscious ( ) Fully zonked

Can I watch TV?

( ) Yes ( ) Heck yes (X) A thousand times yes

How much will I have to get out of bed?

( ) Never ever (X) Maybe once? ( ) Ugh like 3 times

Declutter Your Phone!

You're already on your phone anyway . . . Why not get productive?

THE BASIC IDEA: In case no one has told you lately, your phone is a big, jumbled mess. Give it a digital makeover.

THE WHAT: Do you really need 8K photos of your cat? Chances are no. Numerous apps and even built-in features on your phone can help you delete large files, dump old apps & organize your screens!

THE WHY: More available space on your phone means longer battery life, which is good news if you left your charger in another room and don't want to get out of bed. Plus, everything holds energy, and you don't need to be carrying around photos of your ex. And you weren't using all those budgeting apps, were you?

COZY HOBBY COMFY-COZINESS SCALE

LIKE A KITTEN — LIKE KITTENS WEARING SNUGGIES — LIKE KITTENS WEARING SNUGGIES SLEEPING ON A CLOUD

(Rating: 7 of 10)

COZY HOBBY FYI'S

Do I need special tools?
○ Yes ○ No ⊗ It depends

How cheap is this hobby?
○ Free! ⊗ Cheap ○ Not cheap

How asleep can I be?
○ Super awake ⊗ Semi-conscious ○ Fully zonked

Can I watch TV?
○ Yes ⊗ Heck yes ○ A thousand times yes

How much will I have to get out of bed?
⊗ Never ever ○ Maybe once? ○ Ugh like 3 times

EXTRA CREDIT: Delete old texts. Delete old numbers you no longer need. Super mega bonus points: Go ahead and block that jerk, while you're at it. You know the one.

Learn Some Party Tricks

You better believe you're magic, baby!

THE BASIC IDEA: Amaze and delight anyone, anywhere with your magic skills. When you finally get out of BED, you'll be able to do card tricks, pull coins from behind unsuspecting ears and, depending on how serious you get, possibly even levitate!

THE WHAT: Most magic tricks require just a small few props, and you can practice them from the most magical place in your home.

THE WHY: Having a fun party trick up your sleeve doesn't hurt. Plus, as long as you're near ears, you'll always be able to find quarters for parking meters or coin-op washing machines.

EXTRA CREDIT: Wear a top hat while you practice and make up your own signature magic word. Like maybe *hocus pocus bed corpus*?

COZY HOBBY COMFY-COZINESS SCALE

LIKE A KITTEN — LIKE KITTENS WEARING SNUGGIES — LIKE KITTENS WEARING SNUGGIES SLEEPING ON A CLOUD

(Rating: 5 of 10)

COZY HOBBY FYI'S

Do I need special tools?
(X) Yes ( ) No ( ) It depends

How cheap is this hobby?
( ) Free! ( ) Cheap (X) Not cheap

How asleep can I be?
(X) Super awake ( ) Semi-conscious ( ) Fully zonked

Can I watch TV?
(X) Yes ( ) Heck yes ( ) A thousand times yes

How much will I have to get out of bed?
( ) Never ever ( ) Maybe once? (X) Ugh like 3 times

GREAT MOMENTS IN (BED) HISTORY!

DID YOU KNOW?

British Prime Minister Winston Churchill spent much of World War II in a cozy underground bedroom, where he held meetings, took daily hour-long naps, and recorded many of his most famous wartime radio addresses. Later, Churchill also wrote books in bed, including *The Second World War* and *A History of the English-Speaking Peoples*.

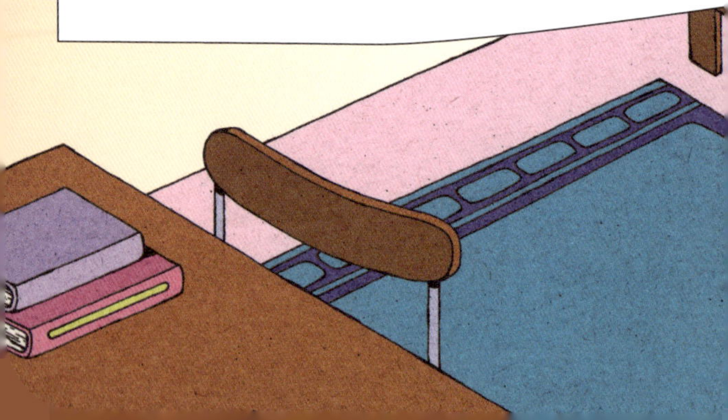

Write Poetry

A poem a day keeps the lack of poems away . . . or something!

THE BASIC IDEA: Write one poem a day in bed. At the end of a year, you'll have 365 poems, which is plenty for a book. Some books only have one poem in them, so your poetry book will be like a million times better.

THE WHAT: Keep a small notebook close by (or type on your phone), then simply begin writing poetry! Now you're a poet and soon-to-be book author. And to think you never had to get out of BED!

THE WHY: You're a deep person and you've got a lot to say. Some of it might rhyme, some of it not, but no matter what, work with what you've got. (See how easy it is to write a poem?) Plus, writing poetry is therapeutic, improves cognitive function, strengthens creative thinking, and more!

COZY HOBBY COMFY-COZINESS SCALE

LIKE A KITTEN — LIKE KITTENS WEARING SNUGGIES — LIKE KITTENS WEARING SNUGGIES SLEEPING ON A CLOUD

COZY HOBBY FYI'S

Do I need special tools?

◯ Yes ⊗ No ◯ It depends

How cheap is this hobby?

⊗ Free! ◯ Cheap ◯ Not cheap

How asleep can I be?

◯ Super awake ⊗ Semi-conscious ◯ Fully zonked

Can I watch TV?

⊗ Yes ◯ Heck yes ◯ A thousand times yes

How much will I have to get out of bed?

⊗ Never ever ◯ Maybe once? ◯ Ugh like 3 times

EXTRA CREDIT: Turn your poems into a real book. It's easier than ever to self-publish these days or even just send your manuscript to the local copy shop to have it printed and bound, and then read it IN BED!

Learn to Be a Remote Viewer

Put your possible psychic senses to use by spying on people with your mind!

THE BASIC IDEA: Remote viewing is a highly desirable skill if you can cultivate it. Essentially, you'll practice tuning into impressions in your mind about an object or person or space that is some distance away from you.

THE WHAT: Find a friend who will practice with you in real time. You'll use the untapped powers of your brain to describe something that is in the room with them or try to determine what they might be wearing . . . you get the idea.

THE WHY: This skill would look really awesome on your résumé. And you'll never have to guess if someone got you a birthday present, because you'll just be able to check with your mind—from bed.

COZY HOBBY COMFY-COZINESS SCALE

LIKE A KITTEN — LIKE KITTENS WEARING SNUGGIES — LIKE KITTENS WEARING SNUGGIES SLEEPING ON A CLOUD

COZY HOBBY FYI'S

Do I need special tools?
○ Yes ⊗ No ○ It depends

How cheap is this hobby?
⊗ Free! ○ Cheap ○ Not cheap

How asleep can I be?
○ Super awake ○ Semi-conscious ⊗ Fully zonked

Can I watch TV?
⊗ Yes ○ Heck yes ○ A thousand times yes

How much will I have to get out of bed?
⊗ Never ever ○ Maybe once? ○ Ugh like 3 times

EXTRA CREDIT: Use your newfound talent for the good of humankind by offering to help loved ones locate lost keys, missing socks, and the TV remote.

Paint-by-Numbers!

If you can match a number to a tub of paint, you can be a masterful artiste!

THE BASIC IDEA: Find yourself a paint-by-number kit, don a beret, and get painting.

THE WHAT: Paint-by-numbers are fun, simple, and affordable. Each kit comes with a pre-printed canvas of some sort, all the paint your project will need, and usually at least one (kinda crappy) paintbrush. (If you really take to this hobby, you might want to upgrade your brush game.) At a minimum you'll need to add a glass of water and some paper towels for brush cleaning.

THE WHY: Who doesn't need more beautiful artwork to gaze upon, either from bed, or anywhere else you're forced to hang out in your home?

EXTRA CREDIT: Actually frame your mini masterpieces and hang them up.

COZY HOBBY COMFY-COZINESS SCALE

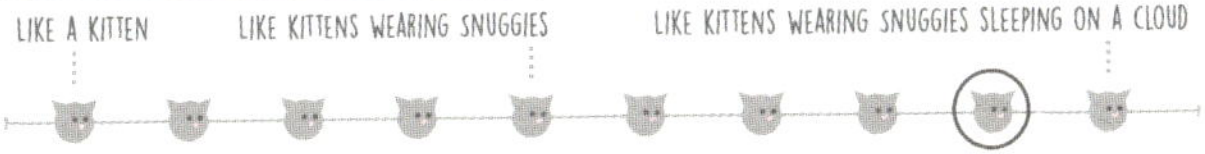

LIKE A KITTEN — LIKE KITTENS WEARING SNUGGIES — LIKE KITTENS WEARING SNUGGIES SLEEPING ON A CLOUD

COZY HOBBY FYI'S

Do I need special tools?

(X) Yes ( ) No ( ) It depends

How cheap is this hobby?

( ) Free! ( ) Cheap (X) Not cheap

How asleep can I be?

(X) Super awake ( ) Semi-conscious ( ) Fully zonked

Can I watch TV?

( ) Yes ( ) Heck yes (X) A thousand times yes

How much will I have to get out of bed?

( ) Never ever (X) Maybe once? ( ) Ugh like 3 times

Build Self-Esteem with Mirror Work!

You are beautiful. You are capable. You are worth it!

THE BASIC IDEA: Use a mirror as a tool to rebuild your self-esteem and heal your inner child, while lying in your cozy cocoon.

THE WHAT: Gaze into your very own windows-to-the-soul (your eyes!), and give yourself heartfelt compliments. You might feel silly, but give it time to work its magic.

THE WHY: There's something truly alchemical about this mirror-talk trick. And your bed is the one place in the world where you're at your most comfy and relaxed!

COZY HOBBY COMFY-COZINESS SCALE

LIKE A KITTEN — LIKE KITTENS WEARING SNUGGIES — LIKE KITTENS WEARING SNUGGIES SLEEPING ON A CLOUD

(Scale of 10; 10th circled)

COZY HOBBY FYI'S

Do I need special tools?
(X) Yes ( ) No ( ) It depends

How cheap is this hobby?
(X) Free! ( ) Cheap ( ) Not cheap

How asleep can I be?
( ) Super awake ( ) Semi-conscious (X) Fully zonked

Can I watch TV?
(X) Yes ( ) Heck yes ( ) A thousand times yes

How much will I have to get out of bed?
(X) Never ever ( ) Maybe once? ( ) Ugh like 3 times

HOT TIP: *Maintain eye contact with yourself and start simple. It can feel amazing to say something as basic as,* "I am human being, and therefore I deserve respect." *Or try a self-pep talk, like,* "I am good at ____________________."

EXTRA CREDIT: Write your affirmations on sticky notes and stick 'em to your mirror. Every time you look in the mirror, do a rep of at least three affirmations. It's like a workout for your mental health.

GREAT MOMENTS IN (BED) HISTORY!

DID YOU KNOW?

Celebrated artist Frida Kahlo spent most of her life bedridden, which spurred her to explore painting as a form of expression and sense of purpose. When she had her first solo art exhibition, in Mexico City, Kahlo had her bed moved to the gallery so she could attend in person.

The bed comprehends our whole life, for we were born in it, we live in it, and we shall die in it.

—GUY de MAUPASSANT

You will enjoy a long and fruitful life. In bed.